Hundreds of

Interesting and Useless Facts

by

Kerry Butters.

I have collected these random facts from various sources on the internet like Wikipedia etc, so they may or may not be true. Now please proceed to reading these interesting random facts.

Hundreds of Interesting and Useless Facts

Butterflies cannot fly if their body temperature is less than 86 degrees.

Neurons multiply at a rate 250,000 neurons per minute during early pregnancy.

Elephants have the longest pregnancy in the animal kingdom at 22 months. The longest human pregnancy on record is 17 months, 11 days.

A female oyster produces 100 million young in her lifetime, the typical hen lays 19 dozen eggs a year, and it is possible for one female cat to be responsible for the birth of 20,736 kittens in four years. Michelle Druggar holds the record for largest human family, having given birth to 17 children.

750ml of blood pumps through your brain every minute which is 15-20% of blood flow from the heart.

The human brain is about 75% water.

Dragonflies are capable of flying sixty miles per hour, making them one of the fastest insects. This is good since they are in a big hurry, as they only live about twenty-four hours.

Flies jump backwards during takeoff.

A housefly will regurgitate its food and eat it again.

Termites outweigh humans by almost ten to one.

A spider's web is not a home, but rather a trap for its food. They are as individual as snowflakes, with no two ever being the same. Some tropical spiders have built webs over eighteen feet across.

More people are afraid of spiders than death. Amazingly, few people are afraid of Champagne corks even though you are more likely to be killed by one than by a spider.

Your brain consumes 25 watts of power while you're awake. This amount of energy is enough to illuminate a lightbulb.

It is impossible to lick your elbow.

Intelligent people have more zinc and copper in their hair.

In every episode of Seinfeld there is a Superman somewhere.

Possums have one of the shortest pregnancies at 16 days. The shortest human pregnancy to produce a healthy baby was 22 weeks, 6 days -- the baby was the length of a ballpoint pen.

Wearing headphones for just an hour will increase the bacteria in your ear by 700 times.

The most poisonous spider is the black widow. Its venom is more potent than a rattlesnake's.

13% of Americans actually believe that some parts of the moon are made of cheese.

The world's youngest parents were 8 and 9 and lived in China in 1910.

Fish that live more than 800 meters below the ocean surface don't have eyes.

Butterflies range in size from a tiny 1/8 inch to a huge almost 12 inches.

Some Case Moth caterpillars (Psychidae) build a case around themselves that they always carry with them. It is made of silk and pieces of plants or soil.

Most household dust is made of dead skin cells.

One in eight million people has progeria, a disease that causes people to grow faster than they age.

The male seahorse carries the eggs until they hatch instead of the female.

Negative emotions such as anxiety and depression can weaken your immune system.

Stephen Hawking was born exactly 300 years after Galileo died.

Mercury is the only planet whose orbit is coplanar with its equator.

The Morgan's Sphinx Moth from Madagascar has a proboscis (tube mouth) that is 12 to 14 inches long to get the nectar from the bottom of a 12 inch deep orchid discovered by Charles Darwin.

Some moths never eat anything as adults because they don't have mouths. They must live on the energy they stored as caterpillars.

In 1958 Entomologist W.G. Bruce published a list of Arthropod references in the Bible. The most frequently named bugs from the Bible are: Locust: 24, Moth: 11, Grasshopper: 10, Scorpion: 10, Caterpillar: 9, and Bee: 4.

People eat insects – called "Entomophagy"(people eating bugs) – it has been practiced for centuries throughout Africa, Australia, Asia, the Middle East, and North, Central and South America. Why? Because many bugs are both protein-rich and good sources of vitamins, minerals and fats.

Grapes explode when you put them in the microwave. Go on, try it then

Ramses brand condom is named after the great pharaoh Ramses II who fathered over 160 children.

Peanuts are one of the ingredients of dynamite.

The average chocolate bar has 8 insects' legs in it.

In York, it is perfectly legal to shoot a Scotsman with a bow and arrow (except on Sundays)

No piece of square dry paper can be folded in half more than 7 times

The average human eats 8 spiders in their lifetime at night.

The Beetham Tower cost over £150 million to build.

The Beetham Tower has 47 floors.

"Stewardesses" is the longest word typed with only the left hand.

An average human loses about 200 head hairs per day.

Mexico City sinks about 10 inches a year

It's impossible to sneeze with your eyes open.

In France, a five year old child can buy an alcoholic drink in a bar

During the chariot scene in "Ben Hur," a small red car can be seen in the distance.

Because metal was scarce, the Oscars given out during World War II were made of wood.

By raising your legs slowly and lying on your back, you cannot sink into quicksand.

The glue on Israeli postage is certified kosher.

In 10 minutes, a hurricane releases more energy than all of the world's nuclear weapons combined.

On average, 100 people choke to death on ball-point pens every year.

Thirty-five percent of the people who use personal ads for dating are already married.

The electric chair was invented by a dentist.

The top butterfly flight speed is 12 miles per hour. Some moths can fly 25 miles per hour!

The Brimstone butterfly (Gonepterix rhamni) has the longest lifetime of the adult butterflies: 9-10 months.

Bruce Lee was so fast that they actually had to s-l-o-w film down so you could see his moves.

A Boeing 747s wingspan is longer than the Wright brother's first flight.

Representations of butterflies are seen in Egyptian frescoes at Thebes, which are 3,500 years old.

Babies are born without knee caps. They don't appear until the child reaches 2-6 years of age.

14% of all facts and statistics are made up and 27% of people know that fact.

Every time you lick a stamp, you're consuming 1/10 of a calorie.

Eskimos have over 15 words for the English word of 'Snow'

Butterflies can see red, green, and yellow.

Some people say that when the black bands on the Woolybear caterpillar are wide, a cold winter is coming.

Americans on the average eat 18 acres of pizza every day.

Banging your head against a wall uses 150 calories an hour.

Almonds are a member of the peach family.

The plastic things on the end of shoelaces are called aglets.

"Ithyphallophobia" is a morbid fear of seeing, thinking about or having an erect penis.

The average shelf-life of a latex condom is about two years.

14% of Americans have skinny-dipped with a member of the opposite sex at least once.

Male bats have the highest rate of homosexuality of any mammal.

A man's beard grows fastest when he anticipates sex.

A man will ejaculate approximately 18 quarts of semen in his lifetime.

Sex is biochemically no different from eating large quantities of chocolate.

Humans and dolphins are the only species that have sex for pleasure.

For every 'normal' webpage, there are five porn pages.

"Venus observa" is the technical term for the "missionary position."

Sex is the safest tranquilizer in the world. IT IS 10 TIMES MORE EFFECTIVE THAN VALIUM.

Samuel Clemens (Mark Twain) was born on and died on days when Halley's Comet can be seen.

US Dollar bills are made out of cotton and linen.

The 57 on the Heinz ketchup bottle represents the number of pickle types the company once had.

Americans are responsible for about 1/5 of the world's garbage annually.

Giraffes and rats can last longer without water than camels.

Your stomach produces a new layer of mucus every two weeks so that it doesn't digest itself.

98% of all murders and rapes are by a close family member or friend of the victim.

A B-25 bomber crashed into the 79th floor of the Empire State Building on July 28, 1945.

The Declaration of Independence was written on hemp (marijuana) paper.

The dot over the letter "i" is called a tittle.

Benjamin Franklin was the fifth in a series of the youngest son of the youngest son.

Triskaidekaphobia means fear of the number 13.

Paraskevidekatriaphobia means fear of Friday the 13th, which occurs one to three times a year.

In Italy, 17 is considered an unlucky number. In Japan, 4 is considered an unlucky number.

A female ferret will die if it goes into heat and cannot find a mate.

In ancient Rome, when a man testified in court he would swear on his testicles.

The ZIP in "ZIP code" means Zoning Improvement Plan.

Coca-Cola contained Coca (whose active ingredient is cocaine) from 1885 to 1903.

A "2 by 4" is really 1 1/2 by 3 1/2.

It's estimated that at any one time around 0.7% of the world's population is drunk.

40% of McDonald's profits come from the sales of Happy Meals.

Every person, including identical twins, has a unique eye & tongue print along with their fingerprint.

The "spot" on the 7-Up logo comes from its inventor who had red eyes. He was an albino.

315 entries in Webster's 1996 dictionary were misspelled.

The "save" icon in Microsoft Office programs shows a floppy disk with the shutter on backwards.

Albert Einstein and Charles Darwin both married their first cousins

Camel's have three eyelids.

On average, 12 newborns will be given to the wrong parents every day.

John Wilkes Booth's brother once saved the life of Abraham Lincoln's son.

Warren Beatty and Shirley McLaine are brother and sister.

Chocolate can kill dogs; it directly affects their heart and nervous system.

Daniel Boone hated coonskin caps.

55.1% of all US prisoners are in prison for drug offenses.

Most lipstick contains fish scales.

Dr. Seuss pronounced his name "soyce".

Slugs have four noses.

Ketchup was sold in the 1830s as medicine.

India has a Bill of Rights for cows.

American Airlines saved $40,000 in 1987 by taking out an olive from First Class salads.

About 200,000,000 M&Ms are sold each day in the United States.

Because metal was scarce, the Oscars given out during World War II were made of wood.

There are 318,979,564,000 possible combinations of the first four moves in Chess.

There are no clocks in Las Vegas gambling casinos.

Coconuts kill about 150 people each year. That's more than sharks.

Half of all bank robberies take place on a Friday.

The name Wendy was made up for the book Peter Pan. There was never a recorded Wendy before it.

The international telephone dialing code for Antarctica is 672.

The first bomb the Allies dropped on Berlin in WWII killed the only elephant in the Berlin Zoo.

The average raindrop falls at 7 miles per hour.

If you put a drop of liquor on a scorpion, it will instantly go mad and sting itself to death.

Bruce Lee was so fast that they had to slow the film down so you could see his moves.

The first CD pressed in the US was Bruce Springsteen's "Born in the USA".

IBM's motto is "Think". Apple later made their motto "Think different".

The original name for butterfly was flutterby.

One in fourteen women in America is a natural blonde. Only one in sixteen men is.

The Olympic was the sister ship of the Titanic, and she provided twenty-five years of service.

When the Titanic sank, 2228 people were on it. Only 706 survived.

Every day, 7% of the US eats at McDonald's.

During his entire life, Vincent Van Gogh sold exactly one painting, "Red Vineyard at Arles".

By raising your legs slowly and lying on your back, you cannot sink into quicksand.

One in ten people live on an island.

It takes more calories to eat a piece of celery than the celery has in it to begin with.

28% of Africa is classified as wilderness. In North America, its 38%.

Charlie Chaplin once won third prize in a Charlie Chaplin look-alike contest.

Chewing gum while peeling onions will keep you from crying.

Sherlock Holmes NEVER said "Elementary, my dear Watson"

Humphrey Bogart NEVER said "Play it again, Sam" in Casablanca

They NEVER said "Beam me up, Scotty" on Star Trek.

Sharon Stone was the first Star Search spokes model.

More people are afraid of open spaces (kenophobia) than of tight spaces (claustrophobia).

There is a 1 in 4 chance that New York will have a white Christmas.

The Guinness Book of Records holds the record for being the book most often stolen from Libraries.

Thirty-five percent of the people who use personal ads for dating are already married.

$203,000,000 is spent on barbed wire each year in the U.S.

Every US president has worn glasses (just not always in public).

Bats always turn left when exiting a cave.

Jim Henson first coined the word "Muppet". It is a combination of "marionette" and "puppet."

The Michelin man is known as Mr. Bib. His name was Bibendum in the company's first ads in 1896.

The word "lethologica" describes the state of not being able to remember the word you want.

About 14% of injecting drug users are HIV positive.

A word or sentence that is the same front and back (racecar, kayak) is called a "palindrome".

A snail can sleep for 3 years.

People photocopying their buttocks are the cause of 23% of all photocopier faults worldwide.

China has more English speakers than the United States.

One in every 9000 people is an albino.

There are about a million ants per person. Ants are very social animals and will live in colonies that can contain almost 500,000 ants.

The electric chair was invented by a dentist.

You share your birthday with at least 9 million other people in the world.

Everyday, more money is printed for Monopoly sets than for the U.S. Treasury.

Every year 4 people in the UK die putting their trousers on.

Cats have over one hundred vocal sounds; dogs only have about ten.

Our eyes are always the same size from birth but our nose and ears never stop growing.

In every episode of "Seinfeld" there is a Superman picture or reference somewhere.

Rats multiply so quickly that in 18 months, two rats could have over million descendants.

Wearing headphones for just an hour will increase the bacteria in your ear by 700 times.

Each year in America there are about 300,000 deaths that can be attributed to obesity.

Many butterflies can taste with their feet to find out whether the leaf they sit on is good to lay eggs on to be their caterpillars' food or not.

There are more types of insects in one tropical rain forest tree than there are in the entire state of Vermont.

About 55% of all movies are rated R.

About 500 movies are made in the US and 800 in India annually.

Arabic numerals are not really Arabic; they were created in India.

The February of 1865 is the only month in recorded history not to have a full moon.

There is actually no danger in swimming right after you eat, though it may feel uncomfortable.

The cruise liner Queen Elizabeth II moves only six inches for each gallon of diesel that it burns.

More than 50% of the people in the world have never made or received a telephone call.

A shark is the only fish that can blink with both eyes.

There are about 2 chickens for every human in the world.

The word "maverick" came into use after Samuel Maverick, a Texan refused to brand his cattle.

Two-thirds of the world's eggplant is grown in New Jersey.

Termites have been known to eat food twice as fast when heavy metal music is playing.

There are more beetles than any other animal. In fact, one out of every four animals is a beetle.

The rhinoceros beetle is the strongest animal and is capable of lifting 850 times its own weight.

On a Canadian two-dollar bill, the American flag is flying over the Parliament Building.

An American urologist bought Napoleon's penis for $40,000.

No word in the English language rhymes with month, orange, silver, or purple.

Dreamt is the only English word that ends in the letters "MT".

$283,200 is the absolute highest amount of money you can win on Jeopardy.

Almonds are members of the peach family.

Rats and horses can't vomit.

The penguin is the only bird that can't fly but can swim.

There are approximately 100 million acts of sexual intercourse each day.

Winston Churchill was born in a ladies room during a dance.

Maine is the only state whose name is just one syllable.

Americans on average eat 18 acres of pizza every day.

Venus is the only planet that rotates clockwise.

Charlie Chaplin once won third prize in a Charlie Chaplin look-alike contest.

Every time you lick a stamp you consume 1/10 of a calorie.

You are more likely to be killed by a champagne cork than by a poisonous spider.

Hedenophobic means fear of pleasure.

Ancient Egyptian priests would pluck every hair from their bodies.

A crocodile cannot stick its tongue out.

An ant always falls over on its right side when intoxicated.

All polar bears are left-handed.

The catfish has over 27000 taste buds (more than any other animal)

A cockroach will live nine days without its head before it starves to death.

Many insects can carry 50 times their own body weight. This would be like an adult person lifting two heavy cars full of people.

There are over a million described species of insects. Some people estimate there are actually between 15 and 30 million species.

Most insects are beneficial to people because they eat other insects, pollinate crops, are food for other animals, make products we use (like honey and silk) or have medical uses.

Butterflies and insects have their skeletons on the outside of their bodies, called the exoskeleton. This protects the insect and keeps water inside their bodies so they don't dry out.

Elephants are the only mammals that cannot jump.

An ostrich's eye is bigger than its brain.

Starfish have no brains.

11% of the world is left-handed.

Rubber bands last longer when refrigerated.

The national anthem of Greece has 158 verses.

There are 293 ways to make change for a dollar.

A healthy (non-colorblind) human eye can distinguish between 500 shades of gray.

A pregnant goldfish is called a twit.

Lizards can self-amputate their tails for protection. It grows back after a few months.

Los Angeles' full name is "El Pueblo de Nuestra Senora la Reina de los Angeles de Porciuncula".

A cat has 32 muscles in each ear.

A honeybee can fly at fifteen miles per hour.

Tigers have striped skin, not just striped fur.

A "jiffy" is the scientific name for 1/100th of a second.

The average child recognizes over 200 company logos by the time he enters first grade.

The youngest pope ever was 11 years old.

The first novel ever written on a typewriter is Tom Sawyer.

A rhinoceros horn is made of compacted hair.

Elwood Edwards did the voice for the AOL sound files (i.e. "You've got Mail!").

A polar bears skin is black. Its fur is actually clear, but like snow it appears white.

Elvis had a twin brother named Garon, who died at birth, which is why Elvis middle name was Aron.

Dueling is legal in Paraguay as long as both parties are registered blood donors.

Donkeys kill more people than plane crashes.

Shakespeare invented the words "assassination" and "bump."

If you keep a goldfish in the dark room, it will eventually turn white.

Women blink nearly twice as much as men.

The name Jeep comes from "GP", the army abbreviation for General Purpose.

Right handed people live, on average, nine years longer than left handed people do.

There are two credit cards for every person in the United States.

Cats' urine glows under a black light.

A "quidnunc" is a person who is eager to know the latest news and gossip.

Leonardo Da Vinci invented the scissors, the helicopter, and many other present day items.

In the last 4000 years no new animals have been domesticated.

25% of a human's bones are in its feet.

On average, 100 people choke to death on ballpoint pens every year.

"Canada" is an Indian word meaning "Big Village".

Only one in two billion people will live to be 116 or older.

Rape is reported every six minutes in the U.S.

The human heart creates enough pressure in the bloodstream to squirt blood 30 feet.

A jellyfish is 95% water.

The world's longest snake (by reliable documentation) is the reticulated python, with a maximum length of, perhaps, 30 feet.

Common Cobra venom is not on the list of top 10 venoms yet it is still 40 times more toxic than cyanide.

The venom of the Australian Brown Snake is so powerful only 1/14,000th of an ounce is enough to kill a human.

Truck driving is the most dangerous occupation by accidental deaths (799 in 2001).

Banging your head against a wall uses 150 calories an hour.

Elephants only sleep for two hours each day.

On average people fear spiders more than they do death.

The strongest muscle in the human body is the tongue. (the heart is not a muscle)

In golf, a 'Bo Derek' is a score of 10.

In the U.S, Frisbees outsell footballs, baseballs and basketballs combined.

In most watch advertisements the time displayed on a watch is 10:10.

If you plant an apple seed, it is almost guaranteed to grow a tree of a different type of apple.

Al Capone's business card said he was a used furniture dealer.

The only real person to be a PEZ head was Betsy Ross.

There are about 450 types of cheese in the world. 240 come from France.

A dragonfly has a lifespan of 24 hours.

In Iceland, a Big Mac costs $5.50.

Broccoli and cauliflower are the only vegetables that are flowers.

There is no solid proof of who built the Taj Mahal.

In a survey of 200000 ostriches over 80 years, not one tried to bury its head in the sand.

A dime has 118 ridges around the edge. A quarter has 119.

"Judge Judy" has a $25,000,000 salary, while Supreme Court Justice Ginsberg has a $190,100 salary.

Andorra, a tiny country between France & Spain, has the longest average lifespan: 83.49 years.

Mr. Rogers was an ordained Presbyterian minister.

In America you will see an average of 500 advertisements a day.

John Lennon's first girlfriend was named Thelma Pickles.

You can lead a cow upstairs but not downstairs.

The average person falls asleep in seven minutes.

"The sixth sick sheik's sixth sheep's sick" is said to be the toughest tongue twister in English.

There are 336 dimples on a regulation US golf ball. In the UK its 330.

"Duff" is the decaying organic matter found on a forest floor.

The US has more personal computers than the next 7 countries combined.

Kuwait is about 60% male (highest in the world). Latvia is about 54% female (highest in the world).

The Hawaiian alphabet has only 12 letters.

In 10 minutes, a hurricane releases more energy than all the world's nuclear weapons combined.

At the height of its power in 400 BC, the Greek city of Sparta had 25,000 citizens and 500,000 slaves.

Julius Caesar's autograph is worth about $2,000,000.

People say "bless you" when you sneeze because your heart stops for a millisecond.

US gold coins used to say "In Gold We Trust".

In "Silence of the Lambs", Hannibal Lector (Anthony Hopkins) never blinks.

A shrimp's heart is in its head.

In the 17th century, the value of pi was known to 35 decimal places. Today, to 1.2411 trillion.

Pearls melt in vinegar.

"Lassie" was played by a group of male dogs; the main one was named Pal.

Nepal is the only country that doesn't have a rectangular flag.

Switzerland is the only country with a square flag.

Antarctica is the only continent on which no Lepidoptera have been found.

There are about 24,000 species of butterflies. The moths are even more numerous: about 140,000 species of them were counted all over the world.

Gabriel, Michael, and Lucifer are the only angels named in the Bible.

Johnny Appleseed planted apples so that people could use apple cider to make alcohol.

Abraham Lincoln's ghost is said to haunt the White House.

God is not mentioned once in the book of Esther.

The odds of being born male are about 51.2%, according to census.

Scotland has more redheads than any other part of the world.

There is an average of 61,000 people airborne over the US at any given moment.

Prince Charles and Prince William never travel on the same airplane in case there is a crash.

The most popular first name in the world is Muhammad.

The surface of the Earth is about 60% water and 10% ice.

For every 230 cars that are made, 1 will be stolen.

Jimmy Carter was the first U.S. President to be born in a hospital.

Lightning strikes the earth about 8 million times a day.

Humans use a total of 72 different muscles in speech.

If you feed a seagull Alka-Seltzer, its stomach will explode.

Only female mosquitoes bite.

The U.S. Post Office handles 43 percent of the world's mail.

Venus and Uranus are the only planets that rotate opposite to the direction of their orbit.

John Adams, Thomas Jefferson, and James Monroe died on July 4th.

Baby Ruth candy bar was named after Grover Cleveland's daughter, Ruth, not the baseball player.

Dolphins can look in different directions with each eye. They can sleep with one eye open.

The Falkland Isles (pop. about 2000) has over 700000 sheep (350 per person).

There are 41,806 different spoken languages in the world today.

The city of Venice stands on about 120 small islands.

The past-tense of the English word "dare" is "durst"

Beetles taste like apples, wasps like pine nuts, and worms like fried bacon.

Of all the words in the English language, the word 'set' has the most definitions!

What is called a "French kiss" in the English speaking world is known as an "English kiss" in France.

"Almost" is the longest word in the English language with all the letters in alphabetical order.

"Rhythm" is the longest English word without a vowel.

In 1386, a pig in France was executed by public hanging for the murder of a child

A cockroach can live several weeks with its head cut off!

Human thigh bones are stronger than concrete.

You can't kill yourself by holding your breath

There is a city called Rome on every continent.

Your heart beats over 100,000 times a day!

The skeleton of Jeremy Bentham is present at all important meetings of the University of London

Right handed people live, on average, nine years longer than left-handed people

Your ribs move about 5 million times a year, every time you breathe!

One quarter of the bones in your body, are in your feet!

Like fingerprints, everyone's tongue print is different!

Fingernails grow nearly 4 times faster than toenails!

Most dust particles in your house are made from dead skin!

Present population of 7 billion plus people of the world is

predicted to become 15 billion by 2080.

Women blink nearly twice as much as men.

Adolf Hitler was a vegetarian, and had only ONE testicle.

Honey is the only food that does not spoil.

Months that begin on a Sunday will always have a "Friday the 13th."

Coca-Cola would be green if coloring weren't added to it.

On average a hedgehog's heart beats 300 times a minute.

More people are killed each year from bees than from snakes.

The average lead pencil will draw a line 35 miles long or write approximately 50,000 English words.

More people are allergic to cow's milk than any other food.

Camels have three eyelids to protect themselves from blowing sand.

The placement of a donkey's eyes in it's' heads enables it to see all four feet at all times!

The six official languages of the U.N. are: English, French, Arabic, Chinese, Russian and Spanish.

Earth is the only planet not named after a god.

It's against the law to burp, or sneeze in a church in Nebraska, USA.

You're born with 300 bones, but by the time you become an adult, you only have 206.

Some worms will eat themselves if they can't find any food!

The world's oldest piece of chewing gum is 9000 years old!

The longest recorded flight of a chicken is 13 seconds

Owls are the only birds that can see the color blue.

A man named Charles Osborne had the hiccups for 69 years!

A giraffe can clean its ears with its 21-inch tongue!

The average person laughs 10 times a day!

The Bible, the world's best-selling book, is also the world's most shoplifted book.

Someone paid $14,000 for the bra worn by Marilyn Monroe in the film 'Some Like It Hot'.

Your tongue is the only muscle in your body that is attached at only one end.

More than 1,000 different languages are spoken on the continent of Africa.

Buckingham Palace in England has over six hundred rooms.

There was once an undersea post office in the Bahamas.

Ninety percent of New York City cabbies are recently arrived immigrants.

It's possible to lead a cow upstairs...but not downstairs.

A snail can sleep for three years.

No word in the English language rhymes with "MONTH".

Average life span of a major league baseball: 7 pitches.

Our eyes are always the same size from birth, but our nose and ears never stop growing.

"Go." is the shortest complete sentence in the English language.

The "pound" key on your keyboard () is called an octotroph.

The only domestic animal not mentioned in the Bible is the cat.

Table tennis balls have been known to travel off the paddle at speeds up to 160 km/hr.

Pepsi originally contained pepsin, thus the name.

The original story from "Tales of 1001 Arabian Nights" begins, "Aladdin was a little Chinese boy."

Nutmeg is extremely poisonous if injected intravenously.

Honey is the only natural food that is made without destroying any kind of life.

The volume of the earth's moon is the same as the volume of the Pacific Ocean.

Cephalacaudal recapitulation is the reason our extremities develop faster than the rest of us.

Chinese Crested dogs can get acne.

Each year there is one ton of cement poured for each man woman and child in the world.

The house fly hums in the middle octave key of F.

The only capital letter in the Roman alphabet with exactly one end point is P.

The giant red star Betelgeuse has a diameter larger than that of the Earth's orbit around the sun.

Hummingbirds are the only animals that can fly backwards.

A cat's jaw cannot move sideways.

The human heart creates enough pressure when it pumps out to the body to squirt blood 30 feet.

The flea can jump 350 times its body length. It's like a human jumping the length of a football field.

Some lions mate over 50 times a day.

Rubber bands last longer when refrigerated.

The average person's left hand does 56% of the typing.

The longest one-syllable word in the English language is "screeched."

All of the clocks in the movie "Pulp Fiction" are stuck on 4:20.

"Dreamt" is the only English word that ends in the letters "mt."

Maine is the only state (in USA) whose name is just one syllable.

The giant squid has the largest eyes in the world.

In England, the Speaker of the House is not allowed to speak.

Mr. Rogers was an ordained minister.

A rat can last longer without water than a camel.

Your stomach has to produce a new layer of mucus every two weeks or it will digest itself.

A female ferret will die if it goes into heat and cannot find a mate.

A 2" X 4" is really 1-1/2" by 3-1/2".

On average, 12 newborns will be given to the wrong parents daily.

There are no words in the dictionary that rhyme with orange, purple, silver and month.

The caterpillars of some Snout Moths (Pyralididae) live in or on water-plants.

The females of some moth species lack wings, all they can do to move is crawl.

If one places a tiny amount of liquor on a scorpion, it will instantly go mad and sting itself to death.

The first CD pressed in the US was Bruce Springsteen's "Born in the USA."

Sherlock Holmes NEVER said, "Elementary, my dear Watson."

California consumes more bottled water than any other product.

California has issued 6 drivers licenses to people named "Jesus Christ."

In 1980, a Las Vegas hospital suspended workers for betting on when patients would die.

Nevada is the driest state in the U.S.. Each year it averages 7.5 inches (19 cm) of rain.

In Utah, it is illegal to swear in front of a dead person.

Salt Lake City, Utah has a law against carrying an unwrapped ukulele on the street.

Arizona was the last of the 48 adjoining continental states to enter the Union.

It is illegal to hunt camels in the state of Arizona.

Wyoming was the first state to give women the right to vote in 1869.

Denver, Colorado lays claim to the invention of the cheeseburger.

The first license plate on a car in the United States was issued in Denver, Colorado in 1908.

The state of Maryland has no natural Lakes.

Illinois has the highest number of personalized license plates than any other state.

Residents of Houston, Texas lead the U.S. in eating out - approximately 4.6 times per week.

Laredo, Texas is the U.S.'s farthest inland port.

Rugby, North Dakota is the geographical center of North America.

Butte County, South Dakota is the geographical center of the U.S.

Louisiana's capital building is the tallest one of any U.S. state.

Hawaii is the only coffee producing state.

One in seven workers in Boston, Massachusetts walks to work.

The "Dull Men's Hall of Fame" is located in Carroll, Wisconsin.

Gary, Indiana is the murder capital of the U.S. - probably the world.

Alabama was the first state to recognize Christmas as an official holiday.

The largest NFL stadium is the Pontiac Silverdome in Detroit, Michigan.

Michigan was the first state to have roadside picnic tables.

No matter where you stand in Michigan, you are never more than 85 miles from a Great Lake.

The official beverage of Ohio is tomato juice.

Georgia's state motto is "Wisdom, Justice and Moderation."

The U.S. city with the highest rate of lightning strikes per capita is Clearwater, Florida.

It's illegal to spit on the sidewalk in Norfolk, Virginia.

The first streetlights in America were installed in Philadelphia around 1757.

The highest point in Pennsylvania is lower than the lowest point in Colorado.

If you were to take a taxicab from New York City to Los Angeles, it would cost you $8,325.

The NY phone book had 22 Hitlers before WWII. The NY phone book had 0 Hitlers after WWII.

In New York State, it is illegal to but any alcohol on Sundays before noon.

There were 240 pedestrian fatalities in New York City in 1994.

Columbia University is the second largest landowner in New York City, after the Catholic Church.

Montpelier, Vermont is the only state capital without a McDonalds.

Maine is the only state that has borders with only one other state.

The first McDonald's restaurant in Canada was in Richmond, British Columbia.

In 1984, a Canadian farmer began renting advertising space on his cows.

There are more donut shops in Canada per capita than any other country.

0.3% of all road accidents in Canada involve a Moose.

In the great fire of London in 1666 half of London was burnt down but only 6 people were injured.

In Quebec, there is an old law that states margarine must be a different color than butter.

The largest taxi fleet in the world is found in Mexico City. The city boasts a fleet of over 60,000 taxis.

More than 90% of the Nicaraguan people are Roman Catholic.

Cuba is the only island in the Caribbean to have a railroad.

Jamaica has the most churches per square mile than any other country in the world.

The angel falls in Venezuela are nearly 20 times taller than Niagara Falls.

Canada is the only country not to win a gold medal in the summer Olympic games while hosting.

The Amazon is the world's largest river, 3,890 miles (6,259 km) long.

The town of Calma, Chile in the Atacama Desert has never had rain.

The people of France eat more cheese than any other country in the world.

King Louis XIX ruled France for 20 minutes.

The most common name in Italy is Mario Rossi.

Greece's national anthem has 158 verses.

In ancient Greece "idiot" meant a private citizen or layman.

Bulgarians are known to be the biggest yogurt eaters in the world.

Czechs are the biggest consumers of beer per male in the world.

A Czech man, Jan Honza Zampa, holds the record for drinking one liter of beer in 4.11 seconds.

Netherlands is the only country with a national dog.

When we think of Big Ben in London, we think of the clock. Actually, it's the bell.

The Automated Teller Machine (ATM) was introduced in England in 1965.

Buckingham Palace has 602 rooms.

Icelanders consume more Coca-Cola per Capita than any other nation.

Until 1997, there were more pigs than people in Denmark.

There is a hotel in Sweden built entirely out of ice; it is rebuilt every year.

Sweden has the least number of murders annually.

Lithuania has the highest suicide rate in the world.

The country code for Russia is "007".

Russians generally answer the phone by saying, "I'm listening".

The U.S. bought Alaska for 2 cents an acre from Russia.

1 in 5 of the world's doctors are Russian.

Antarctica is the only continent that does not have land areas below sea level.

The people of Israel consume more turkeys per capita than any other country.

Nepal is the only country that has a non-rectangular flag. It is also asymmetrical.

1,800 cigarettes are smoked per person each year in China.

Respiratory Disease is China's leading cause of death.

There are more than 40,000 characters in the Chinese script.

More people speak English in China than the United States.

The toothbrush was invented in China in 1498.

Mongolia is the largest landlocked country.

Vatican City is the smallest country in the world, with a population of 1000 and just 108.7 acres.

In Japan, watermelons are squared. It's easier to stack them that way.

98% of Japanese are cremated.

The number "four" is considered unlucky in Japan because it is pronounced the same as "death".

The average Japanese household watches more than 10 hours of television a day.

The Philippines has about 7,100 islands, of which only about 460 are more than 1 square mile in area.

Yo-yos were used as weapons by warriors in the Philippines in the 16th century.

Australian soldiers used the song "We're Off to See the Wizard" as a marching song in WWII.

The Australian $5 to $100 notes are made of plastic.

The Nullarbor Plain of Australia covers 100,000 square miles (160,900 km) without a tree.

Tasmania, Australia has the cleanest air in the inhabited world.

Greenland is the largest island in the world.

The first female guest host of "Saturday Night Live" was Candace Bergen.

In 1933, Mickey Mouse, an animated cartoon character, received 800,000 fan letters.

The Simpsons is the longest running animated series on TV.

The first toilet ever seen on television was on "Leave It to Beaver."

In every episode of Seinfeld there is a Superman somewhere.

The average human brain has about 100 billion nerve cells.

Nerve impulses to and from the brain travel as fast as 170 miles (274 km) per hour.

The thyroid cartilage is more commonly known as the adams apple.

Your stomach needs to produce a new layer of mucus every two weeks or it would digest itself.

The average life of a taste bud is 10 days.

The average cough comes out of your mouth at 60 miles (96.5 km) per hour.

Relative to size, the strongest muscle in the body is the tongue.

When you sneeze, all your bodily functions stop even your heart.

Babies are born without knee caps. They don't appear until the child reaches 2-6 years of age.

Right handed people live, on average, nine years longer than left handed people do.

Children grow faster in the springtime.

It takes the stomach an hour to break down cows' milk.

Women blink nearly twice as much as men.

Blondes have more hair than dark-haired people do.

There are 10 human body parts that are only 3 letters long (eye hip arm leg ear toe jaw rib lip gum).

If you go blind in one eye you only lose about one fifth of your vision but all your sense of depth.

The average human head weighs about 8 pounds.

In the average lifetime, a person will walk the equivalent of 5 times around the equator.

An average human scalp has 100,000 hairs.

The average human blinks their eyes 6,205,000 times each year.

Your skull is made up of 29 different bones.

Ancient Egyptians shaved off their eyebrows to mourn the deaths of their cats.

Hair is made from the same substance as fingernails.

The surface of the human skin is 6.5 square feet (2m).

15 million blood cells are destroyed in the human body every second.

The pancreas produces Insulin.

The most sensitive cluster of nerves is at the base of the spine.

The human body is comprised of 80% water.

The average human will shed 40 pounds of skin in a lifetime.

Human thighbones are stronger than concrete.

There are 45 miles of nerves in the skin of a human being.

Canadian researchers have found that Einstein's brain was 15% wider than normal.

While in Alcatraz, Al Capone was inmate 85.

Astronaut Neil Armstrong first stepped on the moon with his left foot.

Jim Morrison, of the 60's rock group The Doors, was the first rock star to be arrested on stage.

Frank Lloyd Wright's son invented Lincoln Logs.

Peter Falk, who played "Columbo," has a glass eye.

Barbie's full name is "Babara Millicent Roberts."

The mother of Michael Nesmith of "The Monkees" invented whiteout.

Isaac Asimov is the only author to have a book in every Dewey-decimal category.

Shakespeare invented the word "assassination" and "bump."

It is believed that Leonardo Da Vinci invented the scissors.

Adolf Hitler's mother seriously considered having an abortion but was talked out of it by her doctor.

The shortest British monarch was Charles I, who was 4 feet 9 inches.

Tina Turner's real name is Annie Mae Bullock.

Beethoven dipped his head in cold water before he composed.

President John F Kennedy could read 4 newspapers in 20 minutes.

Bob Dylan's real name is Robert Zimmerman.

Sigmund Freud had a morbid fear of ferns.

Anne Boleyn, Queen Elizabeth I's mother, had six fingers on one hand.

Orville Wright was involved in the first aircraft accident. His passenger, a Frenchman, was killed.

The sound of E.T. walking was made by someone squishing her hands in jelly.

Cher's last name was "Sarkissian." She changed it because no one could pronounce it.

Sugar was first added to chewing gum in 1869 by a dentist, William Semple.

Paper was invented early in the second century by Chinese eunuch.

Sir Isaac Newton was only 23 years old when he discovered the law of universal gravitation.

Hannibal had only one eye after getting a disease while attacking Rome.

A blue whales heart only beats nine times per minute.

A cat uses its whiskers to determine if a space is too small to squeeze through.

A chameleon's tongue is twice the length of its body.

A crocodiles tongue is attached to the roof of its mouth.

Rodent's teeth never stop growing.

A shark can detect one part of blood in 100 million parts of water.

The penguin is the only bird that can swim but can't fly.

The cheetah is the only cat that can't retract its claws.

A lion's roar can be heard from five miles away.

Emus and kangaroos can't walk backwards.

Cats have over 100 vocal sounds; dogs only have 10.

A mole can dig a tunnel 300 feet (91 m) long in just one night.

Insects outnumber humans 100,000,000 to one.

Sharkskin has tiny tooth-like scales all over.

Chameleons can move their eyes in two directions at the same time.

Koalas never drink water. They get fluids from the eucalyptus leaves they eat.

A cow gives nearly 200,000 glasses of milk in her lifetime.

When sharks take a bite, their eyes roll back and their teeth jut out.

Camels chew in a figure 8 pattern.

Proportional to their size, cats have the largest eyes of all mammals.

Sailfish can leap out of the water and into the air at a speed of 50 miles (81 km) per hour.

The catfish has the most taste buds of all animals, having over 27,000 of them.

A skunk's smell can be detected by a human a mile away.

A lion in the wild usually makes no more than 20 kills a year.

In space, astronauts cannot cry, because there is no gravity, so the tears can't flow.

The state of Florida is bigger than England.

One in every 4 Americans has appeared on television.

The average American/Canadian will eat about 11.9 pounds of cereal per year!

There are over 58 million dogs in the US

Dogs and cats consume over $11 billion worth of pet food a year

Baby robins eat 14 feet of earthworms every day

In Raiders of the Lost Ark there is a wall carving of R2-D2 and C-3P0 behind the ark

"I" is the most spoken word in the English language

"You" is the second most spoken English word

Spain leads the world in cork production

There are 1,792 steps in the Eiffel Tower

There is a city in Norway called "Hell"

The human feet perspire half a pint of fluid a day

An Olympic gold medal must contain 92.5 percent silver

There are 240 dots on an arcade Pac-Man game

The San Francisco Cable cars are the only mobile National Monuments

Lee Harvey Oswald's cadaver tag sold at an auction for $6,600 in 1992.

A pound of houseflies contains more protein than a pound of beef

The average American works 24,000 hours in their lifetime just to pay their taxes

40% of all people who come to a party in your home snoop in your medicine cabinet

A duck's quack doesn't echo, and no one knows why.

Non-dairy creamer is flammable.

Pinocchio is Italian for "pine head."

There are more than 10 million bricks in the Empire State Building.

And lastly - You can fit 1.3 million planet Earths inside the Sun.